COLOR
YOURSELF
HAPPY
100 POSITIVE PASSAGES
TO COLOR

To Daniel, Almerinda, and Coskun.

Thunder Bay Press
An imprint of Printers Row Publishing Group
10350 Barnes Canyon Road, Suite 100, San Diego, CA 92121
www.thunderbaybooks.com

Published in the French language originally under the title:
101 messages à colorier – pensées positives
© 2014, Editions First, an imprint of Edi8, 12 avenue d'Italie, 75013 Paris, France.

Printers Row Publishing Group is a division of Readerlink Distribution Services, LLC. The Thunder Bay Press name and logo are trademarks of Readerlink Distribution Services, LLC.

All notations of errors or omissions should be addressed to Thunder Bay Press, Editorial Department, at the above address. All other correspondence (author inquiries, permissions) concerning the content of this book should be addressed to Édition First, an imprint of Édi8, 12 avenue d'Italie, 75013 Paris, France

Thunder Bay Press
Publisher: Peter Norton
Publishing Team: Lori Asbury, Ana Parker, Laura Vignale
Editorial Team: JoAnn Padgett, Melinda Allman, Dan Mansfield
Production Team: Jonathan Lopes, Rusty von Dyl

ISBN: 978-1-62686-661-4

Printed in China

20 19 18 17 16   2 3 4 5 6

COLOR YOURSELF HAPPY

100 POSITIVE PASSAGES

TO COLOR

LISA MAGANO
CHARLOTTE LEGRIS

THUNDER BAY
P·R·E·S·S

San Diego, California

Lisa's tips

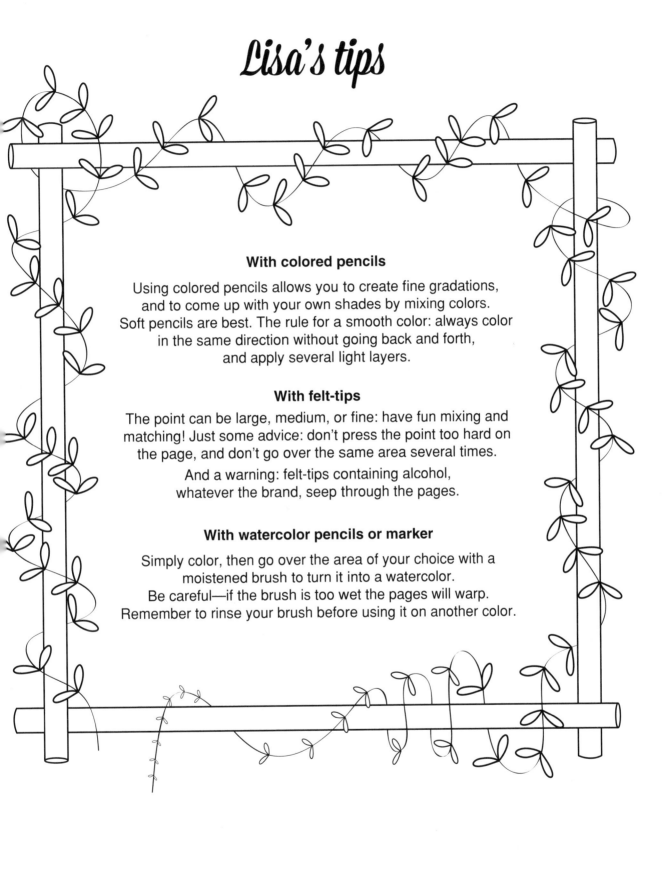

With colored pencils

Using colored pencils allows you to create fine gradations,
and to come up with your own shades by mixing colors.
Soft pencils are best. The rule for a smooth color: always color
in the same direction without going back and forth,
and apply several light layers.

With felt-tips

The point can be large, medium, or fine: have fun mixing and
matching! Just some advice: don't press the point too hard on
the page, and don't go over the same area several times.

And a warning: felt-tips containing alcohol,
whatever the brand, seep through the pages.

With watercolor pencils or marker

Simply color, then go over the area of your choice with a
moistened brush to turn it into a watercolor.
Be careful—if the brush is too wet the pages will warp.
Remember to rinse your brush before using it on another color.

Today's defeat is tomorrow's victory.

The path is the destination. Enjoy the journey.

When you share your happiness, it grows.

Rain is the promise of sun.

INVENT TOMORROW.

Look at the sky to elevate your soul.

THE HEALER HOLDS THE HEALING.

Listen to the silence.

Letting go means focusing on the essential.

EVERY PROBLEM IS A CHANCE TO GROW.

DO
WHAT
you love
TO love
WHAT
you DO.

Only dead leaves go with the wind.

TODAY

I WILL CHOOSE

JOY.

Every life
has a purpose.

live for today,
hope for tomorrow.

THE FIRST MOVE TOWARD ABUNDANCE IS OPENING YOUR HANDS.

Decide to be happy.

Simplicity is the greatest wealth.

Look within for happiness—
nowhere else.

My destiny is my life's work.

A HEAD, TWO ARMS, TWO FEET— THE BEST TOOLS IN THE WORLD.

Your daily life is a treasure. Guard it carefully.

The power of amazement.

STOP WAITING FOR THE STORM TO END; ADMIRE THE LIGHTNING.

When you laugh every day, you're taking good care of yourself.

A REAL GIFT IS ONE YOU GIVE WITHOUT EXPECTING GRATITUDE.

KINDNESS MUST GUIDE ALL OUR ACTIONS.

YOU NEED TALENT TO SUCCEED— BUT MOSTLY COURAGE.

Use your life to become yourself.

What can I do to make others happy?

life smiles on optimists.

I am present in the world.

I breathe, therefore I am.

I am therefore I breathe

THE BEST THINGS HAPPEN UNEXPECTEDLY.

Dialogue can change everything.

You can never express too much gratitude.

Tear down the walls and open the doors of your mind.

KEEP HOPING
A "NO"
IS ONLY
A "NOT NOW."

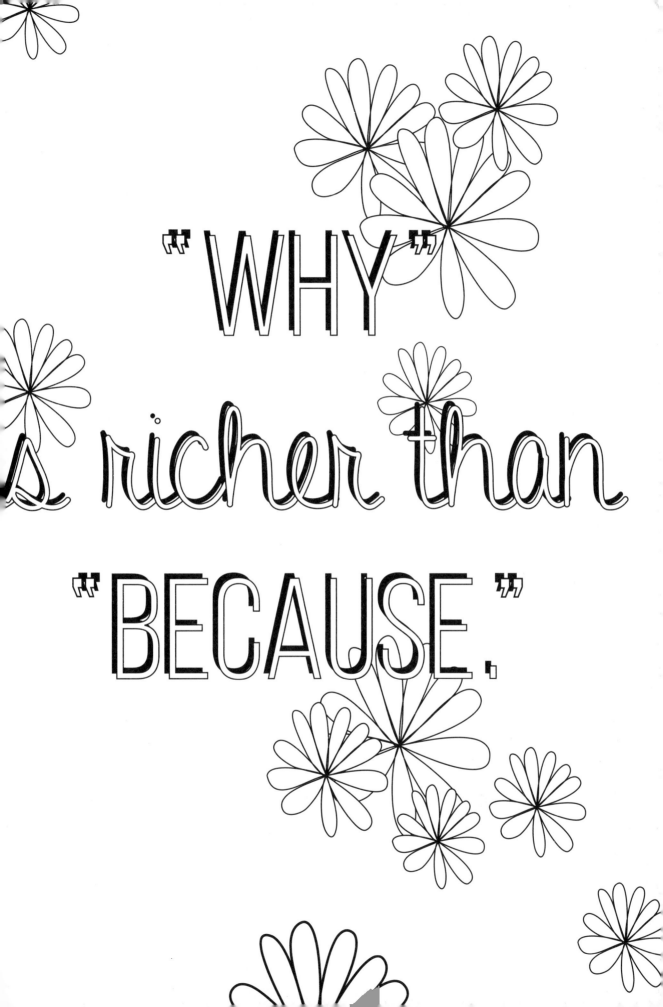

"WHY" is richer than "BECAUSE."

CELEBRATE EVERY TINY SUCCESS.

You travel farther without baggage.

Kindness forges the strongest bonds.

Imagination is an unalienable right.

THE BIGGEST DON'TS ARE THE ONES I IMPOSE ON MYSELF.

Love can
do it all.

Courage can
do it all.

Happiness is before our eyes. We just have to learn to see it.

Luck is the skill to spot opportunities.

Happiness is a state of mind.

Lie on the grass and look at the sky.

FOR A RADIANT FUTURE, TAKE GOOD CARE OF THE PRESENT.

Some things are not important. Move on.

IF
you want to
CHANGE
the world,
CHANGE
yourself.

Smiling is a universal language.

Turn anger into energy.

Small steps
can take you far.

NOTHING is POSSIBLE without THOUGHT, and THOUGHT makes everything POSSIBLE.

It is sometimes useful to do useless things.

Not trying is more painful than regret.

Accepting our weaknesses
makes us stronger.

It is never too late for self-realization.

DO THINGS SLOWLY TO GET RAPID RESULTS.

When you look out for others,
you look out for yourself.

TO CONQUER FEAR, ACT.

Live your life—it's unique.

Say "Why not?" instead of "Why?"

Peace begins in me.

We are nourished by beauty.

Trust is calming.

THE FACE

ACLES

give up

REEDOM.

Turn anger into energy.

Prefer joy to hope.

Don't predict the future, invent it.

The truth will always prevail.

let go of regrets.

The heart speaks all languages.

Make peace with yourself.

TO FEEL IS TO BE ALIVE.

I nurture my inner light.

Eating, DRINKING, sleeping, LOVING, laughing— THE FIVE PILLARS OF LIFE.

We always have a choice.

It is okay to ask for help.

You're the artist!